The Spinning Heart Classroom Questions

A SCENE BY SCENE TEACHING GUIDE

Amy Farrell

SCENE BY SCENE

ENNISKERRY, IRELAND

Scene by Scene
11 Millfield, Enniskerry
Wicklow, Ireland.
www.scenebysceneguides.com

Ordering Information:
orders@scenebyscene.ie.

The Spinning Heart Classroom Questions/Amy Farrell. —1st ed.
ISBN 978-1-910949-03-0

Contents

Bobby - Chapter One

1.   Why does the speaker visit his father daily?

2.   Describe the speaker's attitude towards his father.

3.   Describe his father's house.

4.   "I should have known something was up the day last year when Mickey Briars came in..." Why was Mickey Briars upset? What did he do?

5.   How do the men deal with him and calm him down?

6.   What did you find out about Bobby's work situation and workplace in this chapter?

7. What information do you learn about Bobby himself in this opening chapter?

8. What interests you in the story so far? Give examples in your answer.

9. What was life like for Bobby when he was foreman, before he lost his job?

10. Why did he hide being smart in school?

11. How was Bobby treated by Josie Burke, Pokey's father?

12. Why didn't he stand up to Josie, do you think?

13. How did Triona, his wife, treat Bobby when he lost his job? Do they have a good relationship?

14. "I thought about killing my father all day yesterday." What is your reaction to Bobby's feelings towards his father?

15. Why was Bobby jealous of Seanie Shaper growing up?

16. When did Bobby's father start drinking? What is your response to this?

17. What life did his father choose by drinking, according to Bobby?

18. When did his father stop drinking?

19. Why did Bobby's father, "drink out the farm"?

20.   What was life like for Bobby's mother?

21.   Did Bobby love his mother?

22.   What effect did his father have on Bobby's relationship with his mother? What is your reaction to this?

23.   Describe Bobby when he first met Triona.

24.   What did Triona's friend say about Bobby's family when Triona first met him? How does this make you feel?

25.   Why did Bobby dislike Pokey Burke?

26.   "Having a wife is great." What does Bobby enjoy about married life?

27.   What are your impressions of Bobby, after reading this chapter?

28.   What is the atmosphere like in this opening section?

29.   Describe Bobby's home and community.

30.   Does this chapter give an accurate picture of life in Ireland? Explain your view.

31.   What attitude does Bobby have towards his wife, Triona?

32.   Is Bobby a good choice of narrator? Explain your view.

Josie - Chapter Two

1. Does Josie treat his sons equally? Why does he act as he does?

2. Is Josie happy with how he treated Bobby?

3. What opinion does Josie have of Bobby Mahon?

4. Is Josie a good father?

5. What does Josie think of his daughter? What is your reaction to this?

6. Did Josie work hard as a young man?

7. What made Josie stop drinking? What is your reaction to this?

8. "He never paid in those boys' stamps." What is Josie's reaction to how his son has treated his workers?

9. Why does Josie think he should go to confession?

10.   Why hasn't Josie told Eamonn what Pokey has done?

11.   What extra information do you learn about "that boy of the Cunliffes" in this chapter?

12.   Does Josie sound happy? Explain your view.

CLASSROOM QUESTIONS

Lily - Chapter Three

1.   What does Lily say about Bernie as this chapter begins?
        What is your reaction to this?

2.   "There are rakes of men around here that have called to
        me." What is Lily talking about here?

3.   What type of men does she refuse?

4.   "I only refused a good man once." Who is Lily talking
        about here? Why did she refuse him? How does this
        information add to the story?

5.   What makes Lily look older than she is?

6.   Why does nobody call to her anymore?

7.   Describe her son, John-John.

8.   How does Lily describe Bobby Mahon?

9.   How does Lily describe Bobby's parents?

10. According to Lily, how was Bobby when his mother died?

11. How is your view of Bobby Mahon being developed through each chapter?

12. How did Bernie McDermott treat Lily when he realised she was pregnant? What is your reaction to this?

13. Lily's son by McDermott didn't bring her to his graduation. What do you think of this? Do you feel sorry for Lily?

14. How are women treated in this novel, based on what we have read so far?

15. Is Lily a good mother?

16. Is Lily a perceptive person? Does she understand people well?

17. What kind of life does Lily lead? Does she sound happy?

18. What similarities do you notice in what the characters say about alcohol?

19. Are these accounts emotional?

20. Do the characters appear emotional or sensitive in public?

21. Can you explain the reasons for the difference between the characters' private and public selves?

Vasya - Chapter Four

1. What does Vasya say about the countryside?

2. How well does Vasya communicate with the others?

3. How does Vasya describe Bobby Mahon?

4. How does he describe the Irish men he works with?

5. Does he find it difficult to fit in? Explain your answer.

6. How did Vasya's brother, Viktor, die? What is your reaction to this?

7. What is stopping Vasya from going home?

8. What different things does he enjoy in the Irish landscape?

9. How was Vasya treated by Pokey Burke?

10. What are your impressions of Pokey Burke, from reading the first four chapters of this novel?

CLASSROOM QUESTIONS

Réaltín - Chapter Five

1.   Where does Réaltín live?

2.   Was she tricked when she bought her house? Explain your view.

3.   What do her father's actions when he's in her estate, tell you about him?

4.   Why doesn't she go and live with her father?

5.   Does Réaltín have a good relationship with Seanie? Explain your view.

6.   What happened between Réaltín and her boss, George? What is your reaction to this?

7.   What financial position is Réaltín in?

8.   Do you feel sorry for Réaltín? Explain your view.

9.   Is she a likeable character?

Timmy - Chapter Six

1. What are your first impressions of Timmy?

2. What opinion does Timmy have of Bobby?

3. How do the other men treat Timmy? What is your reaction to this? Why do they treat him this way?

4. Describe Timmy's family situation as a child.

5. Why does Timmy think his sister blames him for her baby dying? Do you think this is the case?

6. What does Timmy's brother, Peadar, intend to do with Nana's cottage? Is this fair, in your view?

7. How do you feel as you read Timmy's chapter?

8. Do you think his employment prospects are good?

CLASSROOM QUESTIONS

Brian - Chapter Seven

1. Why is Brian going to Australia?

2. Does he sound happy to be moving abroad?

3. Why is his mother worried about him going to Australia?

4. Why did Brian's girlfriend break up with him?

5. Is he upset about it?

6. Do you think Brian is honest with himself about his feelings?

7. What rumour has Brian heard about Bobby? What is your reaction to this? Do you think there's any truth in it?

8. Describe Brian's character.

9. What causes Brian unhappiness?

10. Does he have a good relationship with his parents?

Trevor - Chapter Eight

1.   Does Trevor have a good relationship with his mother?

2.   What strikes you about Trevor?

3.   "I'm going to have to take that child from the girl who lives near Dorothy." What is going on here?

4.   What do we learn about Trevor's father?

5.   What is your view of Dorothy, based on what Trevor tells us about her?

6.   How does Trevor's account add to the novel?

CLASSROOM QUESTIONS

Bridie - Chapter Nine

1. Why does Bridie hate County Clare so much? Does this tell you anything about the kind of person she is?

2. What happened to her second son?

3. Why did she stop at the Star of the Sea church? Do you understand her reaction here?

4. How did Peter's death affect her marriage?

5. How does Bridie's story about the death of her son, contribute to the mood of the story?

6. What is Bridie's job situation?

7. Does Bridie have a good opinion of her "second-youngest fella", Eugene?

8. How did Peter's death affect Bridie, in her view?

9.	How did Bridie treat John Cotter, the priest, after her son's death? Is her behaviour here acceptable or over the top?

10.	What does Bridie say about Triona that grabs your attention?

11.	What opinion does Bridie have of Bobby Mahon?

12.	What picture does Bridie give you of her community? Is this a positive or negative picture?

13.	What insight does Bridie provide into Bobby's relationship with his father, Frank?

14.	Does Bridie's account teach us anything about life?

15.	Is Bridie a 'good' person or not? Explain your view.

16.	What is Bobby Mahon like, based on all we've read so far?

Jason - Chapter Ten

1.   What shocking fact does Jason reveal as his account begins? What is your reaction to this? Do you believe it?

2.   What is stopping Jason from helping the police by providing information? Does this attitude surprise you?

3.   "The very minute you've a tattoo on your face, the whole world looks at you different..." How does this detail help form your view of Jason? Do you jump to any conclusions on the basis of these tattoos? Would you expect others to react similarly to tattoos? What causes people to react like this to facial tattoos, do you think?

4.   Describe the woman who encouraged him to get the tattoos.

5.   Did Jason care about this woman?

6.   Did he respect her? Explain.

7.   Why is Jason a "dependent adult child"? What is your reaction to this?

8.   What various conditions does he suffer from?

9.   How did he get, "the post-traumatic shock"?

10.   What is your reaction to this story about his friend Eugene? What does it tell you about Jason's life?

11.   Why did Jason add to his facial tattoos? Is he happy with them?

12.   Why didn't he get to spend time with his son? Do you feel sorry for him here?

13.   How is the community reacting to Bobby's alleged crime?

14.   What opinion does Jason have of Bobby's father?

15.   Why did the author select Jason to tell us about the murder?

16.   Does Jason like Bobby?

17.   As readers, what conflicting information are we faced with surrounding Bobby?

18.   Does it matter that Frank Mahon was disliked by people?

Hillary - Chapter Eleven

1. What opinion does Hillary have of her boss, George?

2. How does she view her friend, Réaltín?

3. Does Hillary's version of events tally with Réaltín's own account? Does Hillary have it right?

4. Based on Hillary's account, how would you sum up Réaltín's relationship with Bobby? Is this what you expected, or did you believe Bridie's rumours? Why is the author, Donal Ryan, giving us conflicting versions of events like this?

5. Why was Réaltín's father concerned about the rumours about her, according to Hillary? How do these rumours add to your view of country life in this novel?

6. "A lot of those culchies are mad though." How does Hillary view people from the country?

7. Is there humour in this account? Explain.

8.   Is Hillary a good narrator? Does she give us a lot of information? Is she biased or objective? Did you enjoy this chapter?

9.   "She never bothers her arse to think about me, that's for sure." Does Réaltín sound especially self-centred, or is everyone like this in reality?

10.   "Aren't you lucky to have a job?" What does this tell you about the employment situation when the novel is set?

11.   Does Hillary sound like a good friend? Explain.

CLASSROOM QUESTIONS

Seanie - Chapter Twelve

1.   How did Seanie Shaper get his nickname?

2.   Describe Seanie's attitude to women. What is your reaction to this?

3.   Based on Seanie's account, sum up his relationship with Réaltín.

4.   Do you like this character? Give reasons for your answer.

5.   What opinion does Seanie have of Bobby Mahon?

6.   "I never told anyone about the blackness I feel sometimes..." Comment on this.

7.   Why doesn't Seanie tell someone how he feels? Is this problem with discussing how he's feeling a personal issue, or part of a wider problem?

8.   Comment on the imagery when Seanie mentions Castlelough.

9.   Do you have sympathy for Seanie? Explain.

10.   "I'd love to really be Seanie Shaper." What do the accounts
       in these chapters reveal about our private and public selves?

Kate - Chapter Thirteen

1. "Dad said a few times I had all my eggs in the one basket..." What common traits do you notice between the characters' fathers? Is this true to life, in your view?

2. "One good thing that happened since the recession started is people will work for less than the minimum wage." What does this tell you about Ireland during the recession? What does this tell you about Kate?

3. What opinion does Kate have of Nuala? Is she being fair here?

4. What is your reaction to learning that Trevor now has a job in a créche?

5. What is your reaction to learning that Réaltín's son Dylan goes to this créche?

6. Does Kate have a high opinion of men? Explain.

7. Do you think the children in Kate's care are well looked after? Explain your view.

8. Does she have a good relationship with her husband?

9. Would you like to work for her?

CLASSROOM QUESTIONS

Lloyd - Chapter Fourteen

1.   Does Lloyd take Trevor's plan to kidnap Dylan seriously?

2.   Does Lloyd have a good relationship with his mother?

3.   "Then I woke up and the kid was standing up looking at me..." What is going on here? What is your reaction to this development?

4.   "...I know that nothing has any consequence outside of me..." Describe Lloyd's mental state, as you see it.

5.   What is solipsism?

6.   Are Lloyd and Trevor good friends?

7.   Are you worried about Dylan as the chapter ends?

CLASSROOM QUESTIONS

Rory - Chapter Fifteen

1.   What view do local people have of Bobby Mahon?

2.   What extra information does Rory give us about Bobby's alleged part in the murder?

3.   At this point, do you think Bobby killed his father?

4.   Does Rory seem happy to you? What makes you say this?

5.   What sort of person is he?

CLASSROOM QUESTIONS

Millicent - Chapter Sixteen

1.   How do you know this chapter is told from a child's perspective?

2.   "I get really sad and I start crying before I know I'm going to." What is your reaction to this? What may be the cause of this, in your view?

3.   How have local people reacted to the kidnapping?

4.   Do Millicent's parents have a good relationship?

5.   What is the mood like in this chapter?

Denis - Chapter Seventeen

1. What is Denis' financial situation like?

2. "Things were building up a long time inside in me." What prevents Denis from talking about his problems?

3. Do his problems sound serious?

4. "I killed a man." What must this mean? What is your reaction to this?

5. Why did Denis want to talk to Bobby?

6. Why did Denis decide to talk to Bobby's father?

7. What happened in Frank Mahon's kitchen?

8. Does Denis regret what he has done?

9. What is your reaction to Denis' remorse?

10. Comment on the mood in the novel at this point.

11.   Are you enjoying this story? What do you like and dislike about it?

Mags - Chapter Eighteen

1. "The way he talks to Eamonn and my niece and nephew."
    How does her relationship with her father make Mags feel?

2. What does the term "Blow-in" tell you about how locals
    view their community?

3. What has caused the rift between Mags and her father?
    What is your response to this?

4. Does anything in Mags' account sadden you? Explain your
    answer.

CLASSROOM QUESTIONS

Jim - Chapter Nineteen

1. Can you figure out Jim's job from the opening of this chapter?

2. "…That fella of the Murphys getting released…" What high profile case is this a reference to?

3. "What's after happening to the country at all?" How does this section contribute to the mood of the story?

4. How has the kidnapping affected Jim?

5. Is he a religious man?

6. "Everyone thought that girl was a blow-in, no one knew she had such a solid link to the place." Comment on what Jim says here and what it shows about how he views his community.

7. What extra information does Jim give us about the murder scene?

8. "But I know in my heart and soul he didn't do it." How would you like this murder investigation to be resolved?

9. How did Timmy help the kidnapping investigation?

10. "I have another strong feeling." Comment on Jim's instincts. How do they add to the story?

11. "I'll have to start putting these feelings into words properly soon." Is this a problem many of the characters have? What comment does it make on Irish society?

12. Does Jim have a lot of regrets?

13. What is the atmosphere like as the chapter ends?

14. According to Jim, Bobby hasn't said he's innocent of this murder. What's going on here? Why hasn't Bobby spoken up?

CLASSROOM QUESTIONS

Frank - Chapter Twenty

1. "I always had a knack for hitting people where it hurt."
    What sort of man was Frank?

2. Are you surprised to find an account by a ghost, or does it
    fit into the story well? Explain your view.

3. What opinion does Frank have of his son, Bobby?

4. How did Frank view his role as Bobby's father? What is
    your reaction to this?

5. Was Frank a good husband?

6. What was Frank's father like? Does this help to explain
    his own behaviour?

7. "Imagine the waste of it, thinking about killing a dead
    man." Do you feel sorry for Frank Mahon?

8. Is Frank religious?

9. What is the mood like, in this chapter?

Triona - Chapter Twenty-One

1. Is Triona an insightful person?

2. What attracted her to Bobby in the first place?

3. What happened Triona's cousin, Coley?

4. What do Triona's comparisons between Coley and Bobby tell you?

5. According to Triona, how did her aunt Bernadette use religion?

6. Does Triona love Bobby? Is she a good wife?

7. Do they understand each other and communicate well?

8. How did Triona feel towards Frank Mahon?

9. Does she understand him better than most?

10. Why has the author saved Triona's account until last?

11. What was Triona's father like?

12. Why has the author brought Triona's father into the story?

13. "...Some people will hate you for your goodness." Is Triona accurate or unkind here?

14. How does Triona view the people of her community? To what extent do you agree with her?

15. Why does Triona speak so viciously of the local people?

16. What condition was Dylan in when Jim found him?

17. How do you feel now that he's been found alive? How does this affect the story's mood?

18. How do you feel as the story ends?

19. Is this a happy or sad ending?

20. What do you think or hope will happen next?

21. Is this a satisfying ending? What makes you say this?

22. Do you think Bobby realises how much he is admired in his community?

23. There is no account for Pokey Burke, or John Cotter, the priest, although both are mentioned in the story. Why has the author left these voices out?

24. What does this novel suggest about parent-child relationships in Ireland?

25. What picture of life in Ireland emerges in this text? Is this representation accurate?

26. How is Irish culture characterised in this novel? What aspects of Irish culture in particular does the author focus on?

27. What view of women is expressed in this novel?

28. Is the world of this text a violent place?

29. Is the author trying to teach us anything in these accounts?

30. Why has the author chosen this style of narration?

31. Did you enjoy this story?

Scene by Scene

Scene by Scene guides are written by teachers, for teachers. The aim of this guide is to be a time-saving resource, helping busy teachers to prepare classes and set homework. We hope this book leads to enjoyable lessons and rewarding classroom experiences, for teachers and students alike.

About the author

This guide's author, Amy Farrell, is a secondary school English teacher from Co. Wicklow, teaching in north County Dublin since 2004.

Scene by Scene Series

Hamlet Scene by Scene

King Lear Scene by Scene

Macbeth Scene by Scene

Romeo and Juliet Scene by Scene

Shakespeare Scene by Scene Volume 1

Classroom Questions Series

A Doll's House Classroom Questions

Animal Farm Classroom Questions

Foster Classroom Questions

Good Night, Mr. Tom Classroom Questions

Martyn Pig Classroom Questions

Of Mice and Men Classroom Questions

Pride and Prejudice Classroom Questions

Private Peaceful Classroom Questions

The Fault in Our Stars Classroom Questions

The Old Man and the Sea Classroom Questions

The Outsiders Classroom Questions

To Kill a Mockingbird Classroom Questions

The Spinning Heart Classroom Questions

Visit www.scenebysceneguides.com to find out more about Scene by Scene Classroom Questions teaching guides and workbooks.

Printed in Great Britain
by Amazon

21009973R00031